LITTLE BIG BOOKS

# RAILROADS AND TRAINS

## DAVID BRADLEY

Editor: Trisha Pike   Designer: Graham Marks
Picture Researcher: Kathy Brandt

Purnell

# 1  HOW IT ALL BEGAN

The first track was laid by the Ancient Greeks. It was made of stone. A groove was cut in the stone. This helped their wagons to run more easily over the bad roads.

In the 16th century, Germans working in the silver mines invented the flanged wheel. They ran their wagons on wooden rails. The flanges kept the wheels on the rails and steered them over the points. This idea was then used in many

**Above: A grooved road.**

**Above: Wooden rails for German wagons.**

**Below: A great contest was held at Rainhill to find the best engine.**

other countries.

James Watt made a steam pumping engine in Britain in 1770. The same type was used in 1809 to make the first engine to run on rails.

The first public steam railroad was opened in England in 1825. It ran from Stockton to Darlington. At first its passenger trains were pulled by horses. The Liverpool and Manchester line followed in 1830. Both railroads used engines built by George and Robert Stephenson after their "Rocket" had beaten all other engines at the Rainhill Trial in 1829.

Before long, steam railroads were being built throughout England, Europe and America. As the railroads took over, the horse-drawn stage-coach soon disappeared.

**Above: A flanged wheel has a rim which stops it from slipping off the rail.**

**Below: In America, in the early days of railroads, stage-coaches and trains would often race each other.**

## 2 BUILDING THE RAILROADS

Railroads were built to carry goods and passengers between towns and cities. As early steam engines were not very powerful, people tried to build the lines as level as possible. When this was impossible two engines were sometimes used to pull trains over the steepest hills.

Bridges were built where the railroad crossed over rivers and roads. Cuttings and tunnels were dug through hills too steep for trains to go over.

Trains often had to cross mountains. This meant cutting tunnels many miles long through the rock. The longest mainline tunnel in the world is the Simplon Tunnel which runs for 12½ miles through the mountains of Switzerland and Italy.

Some of the longest bridges in the world are to be found where railroads cross river mouths. They have to be high, too, because ships need to pass underneath them.

The railroad builder has to be sure that all bridges and tunnels on his railroad are in good condition. He inspects them carefully to see that they are safe.

**Below: Digging a tunnel for a railroad can be dangerous.**

# 3  LAYING THE TRACK

A railroad track consists of two heavy steel rails clipped to sleepers which lie in a bed of granite ballast. This stops the sleepers from moving when the train runs over them.

Until recently the rails were bolted together, but as speeds rose the joints were welded together to give the train a smoother ride. Welded rails are usually laid on concrete sleepers, but the older wooden type may still be seen.

Points and crossovers are used to allow a train to change from one track to another. These are laid on wooden sleepers. The points are changed by electric motors and are worked by the signalman.

**Above: At large stations many points and crossovers are needed.**

Worn track is usually relaid at night when fewer trains are running. First the old track is lifted by crane onto flat trucks. Then the ballast is loaded onto wagons. Finally the hard bed underneath is leveled ready for track laying. Sleepers are then put in place and the long lengths of rail are laid and clipped into position. Fresh ballast is then shoveled between the sleepers by gangs of men. Until the new track has settled down, trains must run over it very slowly.

**Left: Parts of a track: 1. Cast iron chair. 2. Wooden wedge. 3. Steel fishplate. 4. Wooden sleeper. 5. Steel rail. 6. Granite ballast.**

# 4  SIGNALS

The purpose of signals is to stop one train from running into another.

There are two main types. Home signals show red and green lights, and distant signals show yellow lights. When a home signal shows red, the driver must stop and wait until it changes to green before driving on. When the distant signal shows yellow, the driver is warned that the next home signal is red. The distance between home signals is called a section, and only one train is allowed in a section at a time.

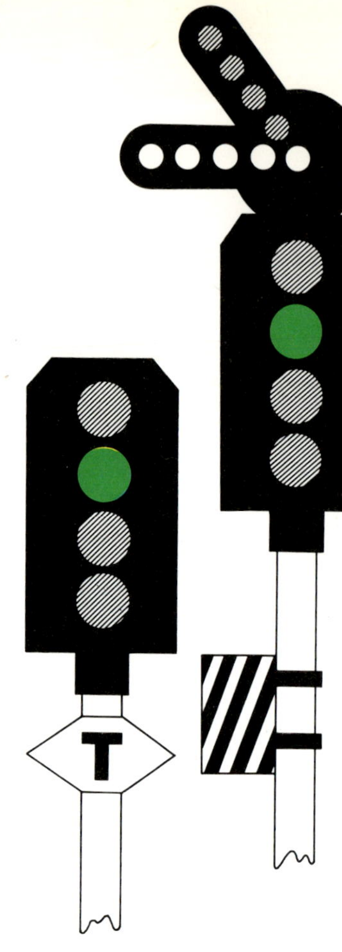

**Above: Two modern colored light signals.**

**Left: Children wait by an automatic grade crossing for a train to pass.**

**Above: Inside a busy modern signalbox.**

**Below: A train speed sign.**

Electric light signals are used in most countries as they are easier to see in bad weather and at night. Signals over a wide area are worked from one signalbox by a signalman. He must make sure that the line ahead of a train is clear before allowing it to go. To make the signalman's job easier and safer, modern signalboxes have small buttons which only have to be pushed to change the signals.

The signalman may also have to look after grade crossings as well. His work is very important. Many years are taken in training him so that the railroads are safe places.

# 5  STEAM LOCOMOTIVES

A steam locomotive works because steam can be compressed into a smaller space (the cylinder) than it takes up. All the time it is compressed it is pressing hard on the sides of its container in an effort to escape. If one end of the container (the piston) can move, steam will push it away. The connecting rod joins the piston to the wheels and makes them turn.

There are three main locomotive types. First, there are tender locos which carry coal and water in a tender behind the cab. Next, there are tank locos which carry coal and

**Above: 1. Firegrate. 2. Heat. 3. Heat tubes. 4. Water. 5. Steam. 6. Piston. 7. Connecting rod. 8. Exhaust. 9. Smoke box. 10. Chimney.**

**Above: A tank loco steams off.**

**Below left: 1. Tank loco.
2. Articulated loco. 3. Tender loco.**

water on the loco. Then there are articulated locos which have two sets of cylinders and driving wheels mounted on one loco. This last type was very popular in the U.S.A. and Africa as it gave the power of two locomotives with only one driver. As a rule, the faster a locomotive runs, the larger are its driving wheels.

The driver and fireman work as a team. The fireman makes steam by shoveling coal onto the fire. He also checks that there is enough water in the boiler. The driver uses the steam to drive the locomotive which, in turn, pulls the train.

# 6 DIESEL AND ELECTRIC

A diesel locomotive has a diesel engine. It is coupled to a generator which makes power for the electric motor in the swiveling trucks. There are usually driving cabs at each end. This saves turning the locomotive around at the end of the journey.

Electric locomotives have no diesel engine. They pick up electricity either from overhead cables or from live rails.

These types of locomotives are more powerful for their size than steam locos. Unlike steam locos, they may be switched on and driven

**Above: A driver speeding along in the modern cab of his electric locomotive.**

**Above: Electric locomotives are powered by electricity either from cables overhead or live rails by the track. A transformer lowers the voltage from the overhead cables.**

at once. Several of them may be coupled together for extra power. Yet they need only one driver working in a clean, comfortable cab.

Electric motors may also be mounted in the coach swiveling trucks along the whole length of the train. When this happens there are usually driving cabs in several of them. Small diesel engines can also be placed under the floor of the coaches. They are then connected to the wheels either through electric motors or drive shafts. These types of trains are called multiple units because their length may be varied to suit the number of passengers.

**Below: A diesel engine (green) powers a generator (blue) which turns wheel motors (red).**

# 7 DRIVER AND GUARD

**Above: First he was a cleaner.**

**Above: Then he became a fireman.**

**Right: Later he qualified as a driver.**

The driver has a very responsible job and much care is given to the training for his job.

In the steam age he started as a cleaner, was promoted to fireman and after many years became a driver. When diesel and electric locomotives were introduced this way of training was changed. All learner drivers now spend some time in the classroom learning how locomotives work and how railroads are run. After that, they spend some

time in the depot working with the locomotives.

When a driver has passed his examinations, he becomes a qualified driver. The qualified driver signs on at his depot each day. Then he reads the notices which warn him of speed limits on his journey. After checking that his locomotive is fit for its work, he runs it to the station to meet his train.

Here the guard joins the train too. Although the driver is in control of the locomotive, the guard is in charge of the train. The driver may only start the train with the guard's permission. The guard sees that all doors are shut before waving the train away. He must not let the train leave the station before time.

**Above: A guard whistles away his steam train.**

**Below: This driver and his fireman keep warm in the cab.**

# 8 PASSENGER COACHES

The first passenger coaches were not very comfortable. They were open trucks without seats. But soon railroad companies were competing for business. Passengers naturally preferred the more comfortable coaches. So, before long, roofs, windows, cushioned seats and carpets were added.

Today, main line coaches have corridor connections at their ends to allow passengers to walk through the train. Electric lighting, air-conditioning and lavatories are all part of modern trains. On some European and American coaches

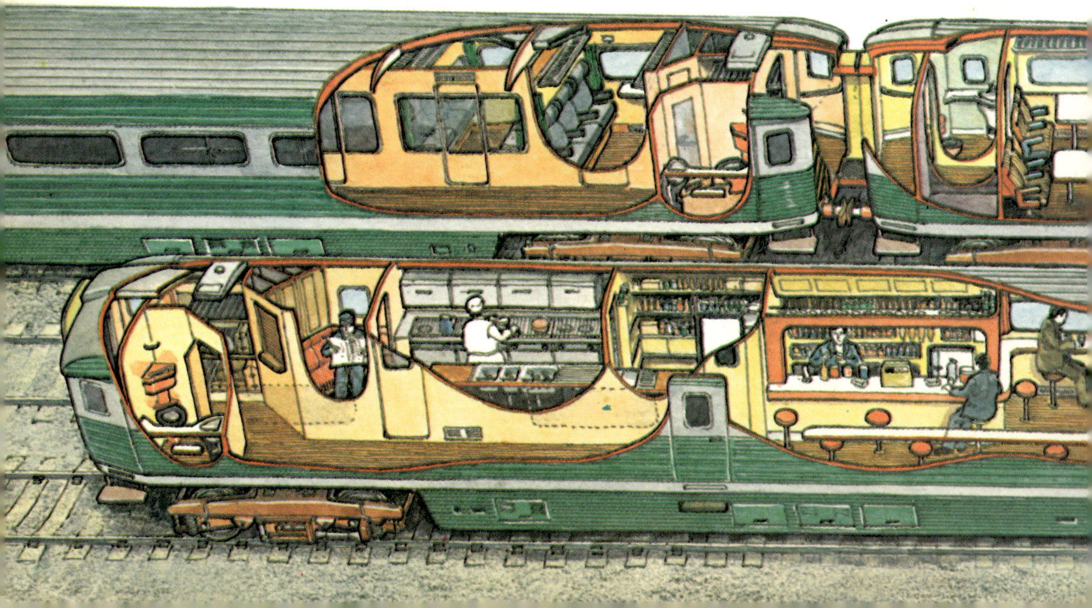

**Above: A porter brings a hot drink to these passengers after they have enjoyed a good night's sleep on board their train.**

the roofs and ends are made of glass
so that the passengers can enjoy the
passing view.

Suburban coaches are built to
carry many passengers, especially
during the rush hours. They have
extra seats and there are plenty of
doors to allow passengers to get on
and off quickly.

Sleeping car compartments have
comfortable beds, wash basins,
mirrors and shaver sockets. In a
kitchen at the end of the coach the
porter makes tea or coffee for the
passengers when they wake up.

**Below: This picture shows the
inside of two kinds of coaches.**

**Above: This
Canadian Pacific
rail coach has a
roof made of
glass, called a
vistadome.
People can sit in
it and watch the
scenery.**

# 9  THE DINING CAR

Dining cars were introduced in the early 1880s. Before that date express trains stopped at large stations so that passengers could eat a hasty meal at the station snack bar.

The kitchen is usually at the end of the car. When several dining cars are used, however, a separate kitchen car may be coupled between them. Although small, the kitchen has electric ranges, refrigerators, water heaters, sinks and plenty of storage space for food. A chef and his assistant prepare and cook the meals for the passengers.

**Above: In the early days of train travel passengers would have to get off the train to eat a quick meal at a station.**

**Left: Today passengers can have a delicious meal in the train's dining car as they speed on their journey.**

**Above: A bar on a European train. Here the passengers can enjoy a drink and a snack.**



**Below: Although small the train's kitchen has everything to make meals.**

Food and drink are loaded into the car either at the dining car depot or at the station. The chef and head waiter check to see that all they need for their journey is delivered.

Tables are laid and meals served by the waiters, who may also serve refreshments along the train and take passengers' orders for meals.

There is also a club car where drinks are served. Comfortable seats and low tables make it seem like a nightclub or hotel lounge. With the dining car and club car, passengers can have a complete refreshment service during their journey.

# 10 FREIGHT TRAINS

Railroads carry large amounts of freight and use huge numbers of wagons, often specially designed to hold one type of load.

Open hopper wagons carry mineral loads such as coal or ballast. They are loaded by crane and emptied through doors underneath into troughs positioned between the rails.

Liquids, such as oil or chemicals, are carried in tank wagons. Milk tankers are lined with glass so that they are easier to clean.

**Above: In Canada marks show what the wagons carry.**

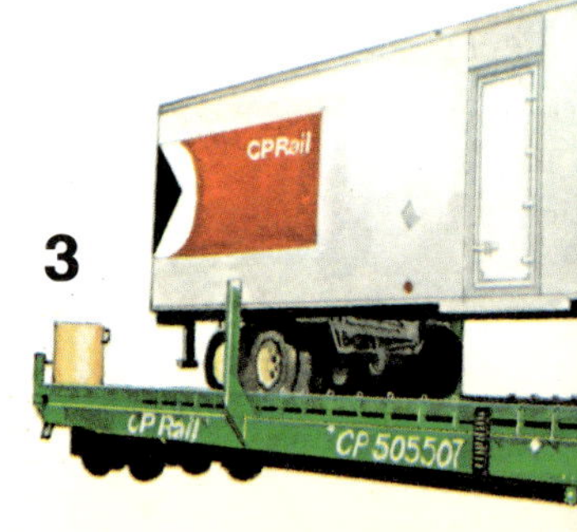

3

Above: A car transporter.

Below: Canadian freight wagons:
1. Covered hopper wagon.
2. Refrigerated wagon. 3. Flatcar.
4. Stock wagon.

Meat, fruit, vegetables and cut flowers may have to travel long distances in hot weather. So they are stored in refrigerated wagons to keep them fresh for market.

Car transport wagons may be used for delivering cars from the factory or they may be coupled to passenger trains to carry the passengers' cars.

As the weight and speed of British and European freight trains becomes greater, more use is being made of swiveling trucks. American freight wagons have always been of the swivel type. Modern freight trains have brakes on all wheels so the guard's van is not needed.

## 11 TRAVELING POST OFFICE

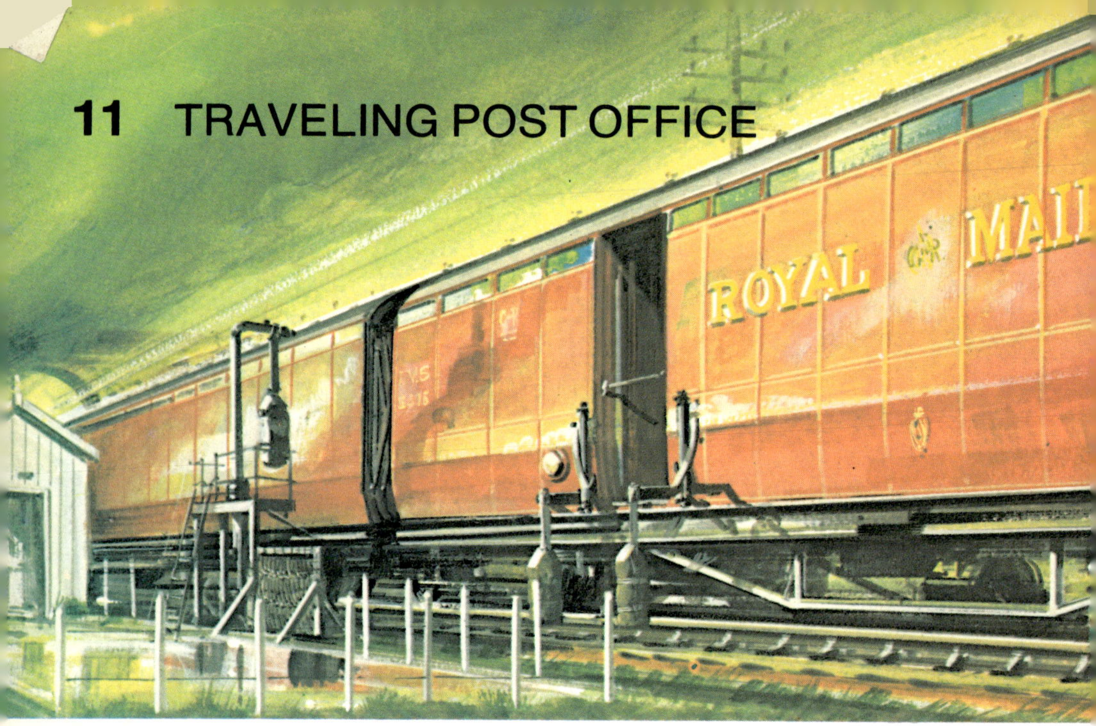


The idea of sorting mail on a moving train came from Sir Rowland Hill in 1838. He was the British Postmaster General at the time. A converted horse box was used for the sorting. The experiment was such a success that a specially designed coach was built later that year.

Even in those early days the coach was fitted with special equipment for picking up and dropping mail bags at small villages while the train was moving. Soon afterward many Traveling Post Office coaches were built. The idea was copied in Europe and America,

**Above: The mail bag was knocked into a net by the passing mail train.**

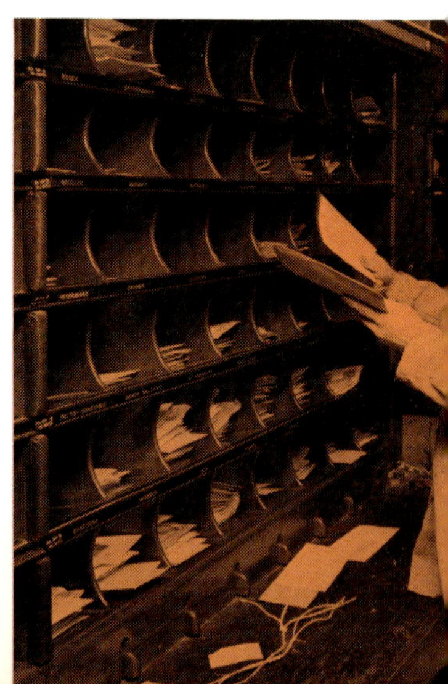

Above: Sorting parcels on board an early Traveling Post Office.

**Below: Work goes on through the night inside a Traveling Post Office coach.**

where the first Traveling Post Offices ran in the 1860s.

Today, mail is loaded on the train late at night. During the journey the sorters put the letters into sacks for the towns they will pass through. The coach has letter racks along its sides and inside it is padded so that nobody will be hurt when the train lurches. The train stops at the main stations on its journey to unload and the mail is sent on to towns and villages by vans.

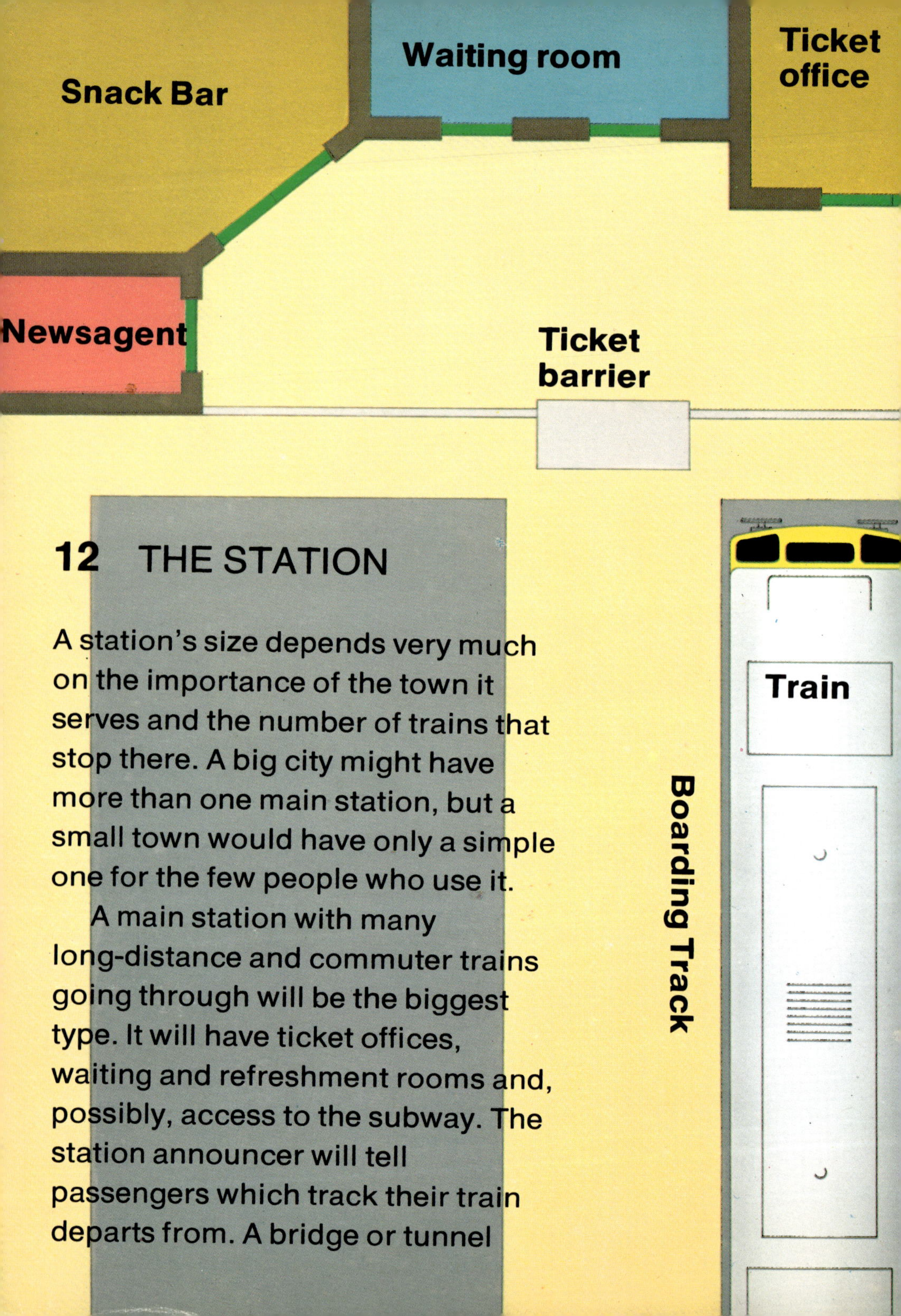


# 12 THE STATION

A station's size depends very much on the importance of the town it serves and the number of trains that stop there. A big city might have more than one main station, but a small town would have only a simple one for the few people who use it.

A main station with many long-distance and commuter trains going through will be the biggest type. It will have ticket offices, waiting and refreshment rooms and, possibly, access to the subway. The station announcer will tell passengers which track their train departs from. A bridge or tunnel

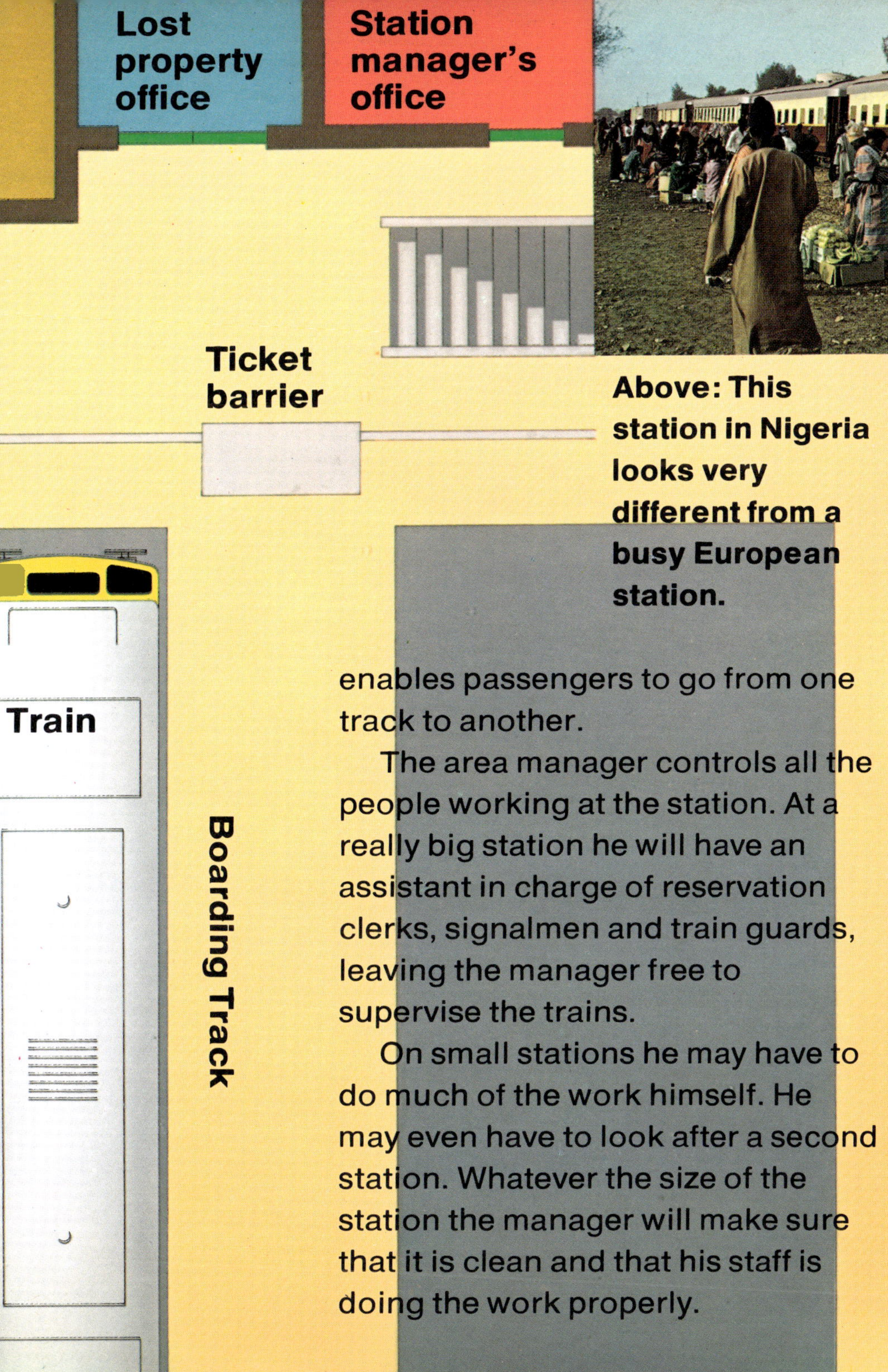



**Above: This station in Nigeria looks very different from a busy European station.**

enables passengers to go from one track to another.

The area manager controls all the people working at the station. At a really big station he will have an assistant in charge of reservation clerks, signalmen and train guards, leaving the manager free to supervise the trains.

On small stations he may have to do much of the work himself. He may even have to look after a second station. Whatever the size of the station the manager will make sure that it is clean and that his staff is doing the work properly.

# 13 NARROW GAUGES

Although most narrow gauge railroads are found in mountainous areas, some of the main lines in South Africa are narrow gauge.

The first narrow gauge railroad was in Wales—the Festiniog. It opened in 1836, and was so successful that others were built for carrying slate from the Welsh quarries. These trains are still pulled by steam. They are open to the public during the summer. Following the Welsh example, many

**Above: There are many narrow gauge lines in the Swiss mountains.**

**Left: The first narrow gauge line was in Festiniog, Wales.**

**Right: A narrow gauge train puffs through South African country.**

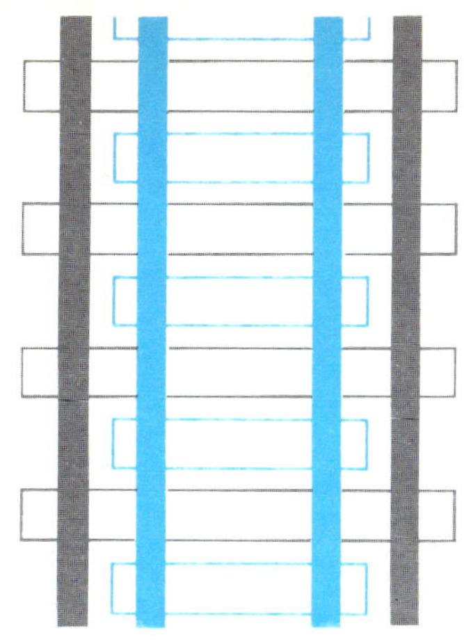

**Above: A normal gauge line is shown in black. The narrow gauge is in blue.**

thousands of miles of narrow gauge track were laid throughout the world.

Switzerland has some of the most impressive narrow gauge railroads, running over the Alps. They are run by the Swiss Federal Railways and also by private companies. They are now all electrically powered. The Pilatus Railway was opened in 1886, and electrified in 1936. It is the steepest line in the world. It slants more sharply than any road. In fact, a road as steep as this railroad would be difficult to walk down.

# 14 SUBWAY

No other form of transport can move large numbers of people so easily across a city as subway trains. By building lines with connecting stations, the whole city can be crossed very quickly.

The normal type of subway is tunnelled by the cut-and-cover system. A very deep, wide trench is dug, tracks laid and stations built. When the work is finished the trench is roofed over. This system is used in New York. In Paris, where some trains have wheels with rubber tires, it is called the metro. Berlin boasts the largest subway in Central Europe.

**Above: Two types of subway railroad tunnel: 1. Cut-and-cover —first a trench is dug. 2. Then the trench is roofed over. 3. A tube tunnel.**

**Left: A Russian subway station.**

**Above: A station on Berlin's subway system.**

**Below: The first electric subway line in London.**

London has the oldest and largest subway in the world. But it uses tube tunnel construction instead of the cut-and-cover system. Tube tunnel trains are smaller than normal subway trains. They run through big steel tubes far under London's streets. The first electric tube railroad opened in 1890, and soon a network of lines was built.

In order to make subway travel as safe as possible many cities now have automatic subway passenger railroads. However, even though a driver is not needed, one still sits in the cab at the front just to make sure all is well.

## 15   IN THE FUTURE

If they are going to stay in business,
railroads will have to change with
the times. The railroads of the future
will have to be streamlined in every
way to carry passengers faster than
any road vehicle can.

In Great Britain, Central Europe
and Japan, streamlined high speed
trains are already running at over
124 m.p.h. In the future, main line
electric trains will be running even
faster. It is thought that 290 m.p.h.
can be reached.

At these speeds the train will be
controlled by a computer similar to

**Above: Trains of
the future may
look like this and
zoom along
concrete track.**

**Above: This streamline train carries travelers in America.**



**Below: The British Advanced Passenger Train is already in service.**

the one in use on the London Underground Victoria Line. Any signals needed will be colored lights in the driver's cab.

New types of track are being designed to cope with these high speeds. Instead of sleepers and ballast, long strips of concrete will have rails clipped to them.

Railroads will always play an important part in the world of transport. As the cost of private driving increases, it is possible that the railroads will once again take the lead from road transport as they took the lead from the stagecoach more than 100 years ago.

# WORDS YOU MAY NOT KNOW

**Chef**    The head cook.

**Commuter train**    A railroad line that mainly takes people who live outside a big city to and from work.

**Dining car**    A coach on a train where passengers can buy food and drinks during their journey.

**Depot**    A place where engines go for repairs and maintenance.

**Flange**    The collar on a wheel, keeping the wheel from slipping off the rail.

**Freight**    Goods carried on trains.

**Hopper wagons**    Special railway wagons which carry bulk goods like cement and which have a special opening in the bottom for emptying.

**Passenger**    A person carried on the railroad.

**Refreshments**    Food and drink.

**Siding**    A short section of track which enables trains to go past each other.

**Sleepers**    Strong beams of wood placed beneath the rails for support.

**Suburbs**    Outer areas of a city, sometimes with a railroad service connecting them with the city center.

**Weld**    A joint made by joining two metal ends with heat.